THE WINE BOOK

THE WINE BOOK

A Guide to Choosing and Enjoying Wine
by
Rosalind Cooper

WILLOW BOOKS
Collins
St James's Place London
1982

First published in Great Britain 1982 by
WILLOW BOOKS
William Collins Sons and Company Limited
London · Glasgow · Sydney · Auckland · Johannesburg
Produced by London Editions/Nicholas Enterprises Limited,
70 Old Compton Street, London W1V 5PA

© 1981 Fisher Publishing Inc.

Design: Nigel Soper and Richard Dewing,
        Millions Design
Editor: Janet Sacks
Special Photos: Peter Myers

ISBN 00 218095 2

Printed in Belgium

R. de Chadelles Champagne;
Chianti Antinori 1978;
Rhine Bear Liebfraumilch 1978;
Christian Brothers' Dry Sherry.

Contents

Introduction

People are becoming more and more interested in wine. This is due to the extensive selection of domestic and international wines. Such a huge variety, however, can be confusing when you want to choose a wine.

There are people who create a mystique about wine. They can give you the impression that if you don't know everything about the subject you can't enjoy it. This is not true! In the wine countries of Europe wine is an everyday drink enjoyed with meals and friends. The same is happening elsewhere in the world, as people learn more about wine and share their knowledge, and wine, with friends.

This book will help you make choices confidently. It provides a simple and clear guide to the wines of the world, so you can choose the kind of wine you prefer. France, Germany and Italy are traditionally considered the best wine producers, but many other nations rival their products in quality and price.

In Europe, Spain and Portugal are gaining reputations for high-quality wines. Even Iron-Curtain countries like Bulgaria, Romania and Hungary export good wines.

However, it is outside of Europe that the most exciting developments have occurred. California has a vigorous industry, backed by research into grape-growing and wine-making technology. Australia, with a climate similar to California's, also makes fine wine. South American and South African wines, too, are gaining acceptance in the world of wine.

After you choose your wine, you will want to know how and where to keep it. This is very simple, even if you don't have a cellar. You'll also learn about serving wine and which foods complement different types best. In addition you'll find information about appetizer and dessert wines.

By reading this book, you'll learn all you need to know to enjoy choosing and drinking your next bottle of wine.

1

ENJOYING WINE

Luncheon of the Boating Party by Pierre Auguste Renoir (1814–1919).
Phillips Collection, Washington D.C.

Some Basics

The very first wine was probably made by chance. One ancient Persian legend says that a grape-loving king stored ripe grapes in a cellar so he could enjoy grapes all year long. Some bruised grapes began fermenting, giving off carbon dioxide gas that temporarily knocked out some slaves in the cellar. One of the king's rejected, distraught mistresses decided to drink this poison potion, only to leave the cellar singing and dancing in high spirits. The king realized that his fruity liquid had the wonderful and mysterious power to make sad people happy. His discovery is something we share to this day.

Our earliest archaeological evidence of wine-making points to neolithic Persia. Writings about wine are dated from 3,000 B.C. By 1,500 B.C. there was a lively wine trade in Phoenecia, Lebanon, Syria, Egypt, Crete and other Middle Eastern nations. Gods, goddesses, legends and songs about wine and grapes were created by different cultures to celebrate the importance of wine.

In the Bible, vineyards are mentioned as valuable possessions because they give both food and drink. Wine is also the sacred beverage for many religions. Because of its alcoholic content, wine's medicinal qualities have been recognized throughout the ages.

Ancient Greeks are usually credited with introducing grape vines into Western Europe. However, the Romans distributed it much farther as their conquests grew. Roman legions occupying Germany, Spain, Portugal and England planted grape vines and made wine. This helped to boost morale and gave the troops something to do when not defending the empire.

During the centuries following the fall of the Roman Empire, monasteries continued to propagate vineyards and make wine. As the power of Christianity spread, so did the culture of wine. Grapes and wine-making knowledge accompanied missionaries and explorers to the New World. Today, wine is made and consumed all over the world.

WHAT IS WINE?

In simple terms, wine is the result of yeast feeding on the sugars of ripe grapes in the presence of air. Yeast is a living, cellular organism. It naturally occurs on ripe grapes as the thin, waxy coating called the *bloom*.

After the skin of the grape breaks, the multitude of tiny yeast cells on the skin begins reacting with the sugars in the juice, turning it to alcohol. In addition, the yeast cells also produce carbon dioxide gas. This makes the crushed grapes bubbly and frothy during the process. You can make wine from any fruit. But with fruits other than grapes you have to add sugar to help the yeast cells. Only grapes produce enough sugar for this reaction to occur naturally.

Yeast action on the grapes is called *fermentation*. If crushed grapes are left to ferment naturally, the yeast usually consumes all of the sugar available, giving it an alcoholic concentration from about 10 to 13%. This makes an unsweet wine described as *dry*.

Wine makers vary this basic process to create different kinds of wines. For example, if all of the carbon dioxide gas created during fermentation does not escape, the wine is fizzy. This is how sparkling wines and champagne are made.

If the sugar content of the grapes is very high, the yeast can't consume all of it before being poisoned by the high concentration of alcohol produced—about 15%. This makes a sweet wine with a high alcoholic content.

Temperature control is critical in fine wine-making. If the wine sours due to improper temperature control, vinegar results. If the residue of crushed grapes remains in the new wine, it affects the wine's flavor and appearance. Some grapes are fermented with skins, some aren't.

After fermentation, some wines are bottled, and others are stored and aged in wooden casks. It is not enough to let wine make itself—it needs some help from man to become its best.

Below: This is a detail from the 12th century B.C. tomb of Nakht at Thebes. Shown is grape gathering at the arbor.

Below, opposite page: Ripe grapes ready to become wine are cut from the vine.

Sherry is usually sold in a heavy, broad-shouldered bottle with a long neck.

Red and white Burgundy come in green bottles with sloping shoulders.

A bottle of claret has a square shoulder and is made of green glass.

German wine bottles are tall; green for Mosel, brown for Rhine.

Champagne bottles are thick and sturdy to withstand pent-up pressure.

Loire Valley wines come in slimmer and paler bottles than Burgundies.

Chianti is available in a straw-covered flask, called *fiasco*.

How Wine is Made

To make the extensive variety of wines available, wine makers have developed special techniques for different grapes and regions. This makes the world of wine an exciting and never-ending source of pleasure.

RED WINES

Making red wine is easy to understand. Essentially, the colors and distinctive tastes of red wines are due to the skins of the grape fermenting with the grape juice. This mixture of skins, juice and seeds is called *must*.

Grape Picking and Crushing—The red grape varieties that become red wines are picked when the grower thinks they are fully ripe. They are quickly taken to the winery and put into a crushing machine. Speed is vital to ensure the ripe grapes are in prime condition and do not begin to ferment too early. Some winemakers remove the stalks from the grape bunches at this stage.

After grapes are crushed, they begin fermenting in a fermentation vat. It may be made of stainless steel, or wood or cement lined with glass or porcelain. Yeast cells that were on the grape skins go to work to convert the sugar to alcohol. The mixture begins to foam and froth as it ferments, liberating carbon dioxide gas. In some areas the native yeasts on the grapes do not give best results, so other specially prepared yeasts are added to the vat.

During fermentation the grape skins release color and *tannic acid*. This gives red wine an astringent taste also described as *harsh* or *tart*. Tannic acid is in all red wines. The wine maker controls the amount of tannic acid in the wine by controlling how long the grape skins ferment with the juice.

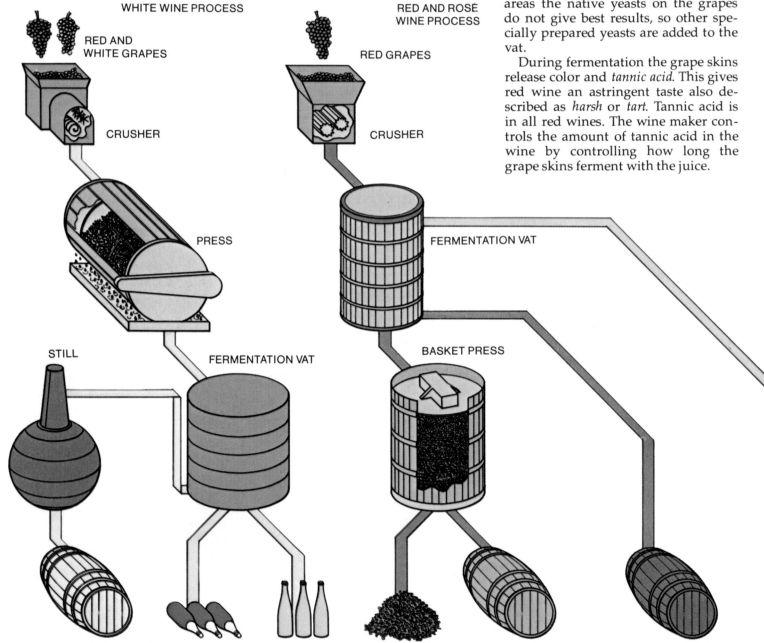

WHITE WINE PROCESS

RED AND WHITE GRAPES

CRUSHER

PRESS

STILL

FERMENTATION VAT

RED AND ROSE WINE PROCESS

RED GRAPES

CRUSHER

FERMENTATION VAT

BASKET PRESS

Brandy is made by distilling white wine or *marc*. It is aged in wooden casks.

Champagne is white wine bottled after its first fermentation. It ferments a second time in the bottle.

White wine is rarely aged in wood. Usually, it is bottled after fermentation to keep it tasting young and fresh.

Marc is distilled from the residue of skins, seeds and stalks after grapes are pressed.

Press wine is made by pressing residue skins that have already been pressed. It is a coarse wine.

Fine red wines are aged in wooden barrels after fermentation.

Cellaring—Wines that are to be consumed soon are *pressed* quickly before much tannic acid is released by the skins, stalks, and seeds. The must is squeezed to release fermented juices. The pressed wine continues fermenting in a secondary vat without the skins and stalks. This makes them drinkable without aging.

Fine wines are processed to have the most tannic acid. This promotes a dark, rich color. Proper aging mellows the wine and makes it most drinkable years later. Fine red wines are always stored in wooden casks that impart additional flavor to the wine and allow air to seep in and subtly alter it.

While the wines mature, they are usually *racked* one or more times. This is transferring the wine through a pipe to another cask. Because sediment is left behind with each transfer, the wine has a brighter appearance after each racking.

After aging in wood, the wine is bottled. It continues to age and improve in the bottle when properly stored.

WHITE WINES

White wine is made from either white or red grapes. Grape juice that becomes white wine is not fermented with skins.

Grape Picking and Pressing—Soon after being picked, the stalks of ripe grapes are removed. Then the grapes

The diagrams on the opposite page show wine-making processes. White wine at far left, red wine on the right.

Rosé wine gets its color from grape skins allowed to ferment with grape juice for a short time.

These ripe grapes show natural yeasts, called *bloom*, on their skins.

are pressed. Stalks have some tannic acid and other bitter-tasting chemicals that are undesirable in delicate white wine. Under pressure, the grape juice runs out. The seeds remain unbroken. Like stalks, grape seeds can add bitterness to wine.

Fermentation—Juice runs from the press into a fermentation vat. For white wines, most modern wineries use a stainless steel vat because its temperature can be carefully controlled. The grapes ferment as described earlier.

Cellaring—Most white wines are at their best when young and fresh. The aim of the wine maker is to preserve this freshness by avoiding contact with air, which ages wine. This aging process is desirable with many red wines because it improves flavor. But with very few exceptions, this type of aging makes white wine dull and flat.

In the cellar, white wines are stored in cool conditions and filtered to remove any trace of sediment that could affect their attractive color. Some white wines are best when consumed *young*, within a few months after bottling. Most others are best when aged for a year or two under proper conditions.

PINK WINES

Pink, or *rosé*, wines are pale red wines. They are usually made by leaving the grape skins in contact with the

juice for a very short time, often less than a day. This gives just enough color to turn the wine pink, but not deep red. The brief contact with the skins also gives additional flavor. The wines are then processed in the same way as white wines.

An alternate method is to blend a little red wine with white until a desirable mixture is obtained. This method is not used for the finest rosé wines, but many very drinkable pink wines are made this way.

OTHER WINES

Like a good farmer, the wine maker knows how to make the most of what is produced. Nothing involved in the wine-making process goes to waste.

Press Wine—After fermentation and pressing, there is always a residue of skins left in the vat. In the case of white wine, the skins are not part of the fermentation process. Using the same press that 'squeezes' the juice for white wine, the wine maker can press all the residue of skins, seeds and stalks to make *press wine*. It ferments in the usual way, but is not of top quality. The stalks can give this wine a bitter flavor.

Brandy—Brandy is a distilled spirit like vodka, gin or whisky. The difference is that it is made from wine, not grain or potatoes. The name *brandy* is derived from an old Dutch word that literally means *burnt wine*, which gives a clue to the way it is made.

Brandy can be made from either low-quality white wine or the residue left after pressing the grapes. The wine or residue is heated in a specially designed container until it evaporates. The alcoholic vapor given off is collected and cooled. This process is called *distillation*. The condensed liquid is then redistilled to remove impurities. The result is a white spirit that goes into wooden casks.

After several years, the wood gives the white spirit a brown color and imparts a pungent flavor. Much of the young brandy evaporates through the porous wood, so the brandy must be replenished with extra spirit. This gradual evaporation concentrates the flavor of the brandy until the day it is transferred to bottles for shipment. In Cognac, the French region that produces fine brandy, the evaporated spirit is called ''the angel's share.''

Tasting Wine

Wine tasters have a habit of using elaborate phrases to describe their favorite wines. One well-known example is summed up in a James Thurber cartoon with the caption:

"It is a naive domestic Burgundy without any breeding, but I think you'll be amused by its presumption."

The trick to wine tasting is to ignore the fancy phrases. I suggest you use a small notebook to record your impressions of different wines. Take the notebook with you when you dine out or go to wine-tasting parties. Write down everything you can think of about the wine, even if it seems trivial. For example, if a white Burgundy reminds you of your dog after it has been out on a wet day, write it down. Memory is the key to wine-tasting, and notes like these help to jog your memory when you consider trying that same wine again. Refer to the notebook when buying wine.

Traditionally, the wine taster divides his notes into the following categories.

1) Observe the color and clarity of the wine by viewing it in front of light. Color helps indicate the age of the wine.

2) Swirl the wine in the glass to release the bouquet.

A silver *tastevin* is used by professional wine tasters. It is small, unbreakable, and shows the color of the wine well.

APPEARANCE

The wine taster will ask, "Is the wine clear and bright, and what is its color?" White wines can be slightly greenish, a pale yellow, deep gold, or similar. Red wines are often deep purple when young, becoming ruby or garnet. Even later they become brick-red color after aging in wooden casks. The older the wine—whether red, white or rosé—the browner it looks. Generally, young wines do not have a brown cast.

The color of a wine may remind you of jewels. A flawed wine, like a second-rate gem, is cloudy and not brilliant. Any sediment in a red wine should be settled in the bottom of the bottle. A white wine should never show sediment.

BOUQUET

The bouquet, or aroma, of a wine is the truest test of its quality. Classifying an aroma can be difficult. An unpleasant aroma implies a wine of dubious quality. A wine that was stored in musty old casks will smell like rotten mushrooms. A wine with a poor cork will smell like wet sawdust. The odor of rotten cabbage can mean that the wine maker was too liberal in his use of sulfur dioxide as a preservative.

Conversely, a subtle and pleasant scent promises a tasty wine. A fine

3) Smell the wine. The aroma will indicate if the wine has spoiled or promises a good flavor.

4) When tasting the wine, let the wine stay in your mouth for a while before you swallow it. Then note the aftertaste.

young French Beaujolais smells of rose petals. A vintage champagne like buttered toast. One French wine taster I overheard claimed that claret smells like an expensive fur coat.

TASTE

The taste of the wine should confirm its bouquet. If its aroma was fresh and fruity, it should taste slightly acidic. To detect acidity, think of lemon juice or a tart apple.

If the taste of a white wine is sharp enough to make your mouth pucker, it could have too much acid, or an excess of one type called *malic acid*. With red wines, mouth puckering means tannic acid. In time, this taste mellows and becomes less harsh as the wine ages. It blends in with the fruity flavor of the young wine.

Because there are few words to describe taste, be creative when describing a wine. If it is not sweet, sour or bitter, you will have to compare it with a familiar-tasting food or drink, or find more poetic expressions.

FINISH AND BALANCE

Both of these words are used by professional wine tasters to confound the ordinary drinker. *Finish* describes the taste remaining in your mouth after drinking wine. A heavy, alcoholic wine will be *rich* and *full-bodied*. The

taste will stay with you for some time after swallowing. This is called a *long finish*.

Conversely, a *young, light* white wine such as a Mosel may have a delicious flavor that fades rapidly. The flavor of a wine that has grown old will disappear from your mouth quickly. A very young, coarse wine will have a powerful flavor but might spoil your appetite. These have a *short finish*.

The ideal wine is called *balanced*. This term implies the "right" combination of tannic acid, sweetness, fruit flavor, and other characteristics. Basically, it means that the wine is true to itself. For example, the true style of a

Mosel wine is always fruity, low in alcohol, fresh and acidic. A good Mosel will have all these qualities, but none to excess—it will be balanced. An out-of-balance wine can have too much sugar, too much acid, too much tannin, too much alcohol, or a combination of these.

THE WINE-TASTING PARTY

A wine-tasting party is a good way to try many different wines of the world. It is great fun and an efficient way to learn about the qualities of many wines. Invite a small group of friends—they don't have to be experts. Ask each to bring a bottle, such as a favorite wine or one they want to try for the first time.

Having a theme to the party is useful. You can try white wines from one region, red wines from another, or compare French and California wines.

Always taste from dry to sweet. Try the youngest wines first, otherwise one wine may mask the flavor of the next.

See pages 20 and 21 for tips on serving wine. You may want to cover the labels and merely mark each bottle with a number. Evaluate each wine when you taste it and compare your impressions with those of your friends when you check your results against the label.

You don't have to spit out the wine after tasting each glass, but don't drink too much because it can dull the taste-buds. Smoking is not advisable because it hides the subtle scent of wine, as does strong perfume. Serve bread or unsalted crackers and water so you can cleanse your palate between tastes. Save the cheese and salad for later to accompany a chosen bottle or two.

Wine	Appearance (3)	Bouquet (5)	Taste (5)	Finish/ Balance (7)	Comments	Total (20)
California Cabernet Sauvignon 1980	Ruby color, bright. (3)	Fruity, rich. (4)	Full-bodied, velvety. (4)	Long finish, good balance. (6)	A well-made wine with several years to age.	17
Château Margaux 1975	Garnet color, bright. (3)	Complex, full bouquet. (4)	Powerful, dry. (4)	Long finish, fine balance. (7)	Exceptional wine with many years of life.	18

A *tasting card* like this one is a valuable record of the wines you've tasted. Score the wine in each category. The maximum points are shown under each heading. A superb wine rates 19 or 20 points. An inexpensive, well-balanced wine rates 16 or 17 points.

Glasses

As with wines, there are many styles of wine glasses available. Choosing the right glass for a certain wine lets you appreciate the way the wine looks. In some cases, it promotes a flavorful bouquet. In any case, the glass you select should complement the wine and enrich the wine-tasting experience.

TASTER'S GLASS

All wine glasses should be clear and without any engraving or etching. They should be made of glass or crystal as thin as possible, with a fine rim. So you can savor the bouquet of the wine, the shape of the glass should taper slightly toward the top. The stem should be long for holding the wine up to the light. The base should be solid for setting down the glass.

A typical tasting glass holds about 10 fluid ounces when full. However, no wine glass should ever be filled to the top because this would prevent you from swirling the wine in the glass to develop the bouquet.

DRINKER'S GLASS

There is no set size for any drinking glass. The average holds about 10 fluid ounces, but any size will do, provided the glass is clear and has a stem. With wine glasses that open out at the top into a trumpet shape, the fragrance of the wine is especially apparent, but does not last for long.

It is possible to use a tasting glass for drinking too, but many people prefer to have slightly larger glasses for drinking red wine, slightly smaller for white. The reason is that red wines respond to contact with the air, but white wines do not usually benefit from "breathing."

The rounded, balloon-shaped glass is used for serving Burgundy and similar full-bodied, dry red wines. German wines from the Rhine and Mosel are often offered in tall glasses with green or brown stems and small bowls. These are purely decorative.

Many people understandably choose fine crystal glasses for serving their best wines. The beauty of these glasses shows off a fine wine, but you should avoid cut crystal. The elaborate design hides the color of the wine. Use

The tulip-shaped champagne glass or *flûte* has a hollow stem, so bubbles last longer than they do in a saucer shaped *coupe*.

German wines are often served in glasses with this shape. Sometimes the glass is colored.

A balloon glass holds about twice as much wine as an average wine glass.

Traditionally, this glass is used for Alsatian wines.

Paris goblet is a simple glass ideal for everyday wine.

these for vermouth or sherry served with ice.

CHAMPAGNE GLASS

Traditionally, champagne for celebrations is served in flat dish-shaped glasses. This shape shows the bubbles well, but also means the bubbles will soon be gone. Better glasses are lovely *flûtes*, which are slim, tall glasses. Some flûtes have a diamond cut in the hollowed-out stem, causing the bubbles to rise in a single stream from that point.

APPETIZER WINES

Vermouth is served either straight in a simple wine glass, or over ice in a cocktail tumbler. Sherry can be served in a special, short-stemmed tapered glass that concentrates the bouquet of the drink. This isn't necessary if you serve sherry over ice in a small tumbler.

DESSERT WINES

Dessert wines like port and madeira are usually served in a short-stemmed glass with a smaller capacity than one used for table wines. Because dessert wines are very sweet, only a small amount is served. Fine, sweet white wines like Sauternes are also served in a small wine glass.

WASHING GLASSES

Many wine connoisseurs never allow detergent to come in contact with their tasting glasses. For tasting purposes, glasses are always washed with very hot water, then drained on a clean linen cloth or suspended in a rack to dry. Using a drying cloth may give glasses a hint of unwanted flavor. For everyday drinking glasses, however, dish-washing detergent is OK.

STORING GLASSES

Many tasters store their glasses sus-pended in racks above a sink, but glasses may also be stored on shelves in a cupboard. Be sure they are not stored near any polished wood or foods with strong flavors. These aromas can taint the flavor of the wine served in the glass.

A traditional hock glass has a stout, knobbled stem of brown glass that reflects color into the pale wine.

A half-full copita is just right for sherry, port, madeira and other appetizer and dessert wines.

A taster's glass is also elegant enough for using at the table.

Storing Wine

If you observe some simple rules and conditions for storage, you can easily keep wines for a long time.

STORAGE CONDITIONS

An underground cellar is practical and attractive. However, few people today are lucky enough to own a cellar and must make do with a cupboard, closet, or corner of a garage that has the following conditions:

Temperature—A constant temperature of about 55F (13C) is ideal. A variable temperature between 45F and 65F (7C and 18C) is acceptable if the change is slow and steady.

Vibration—Minimize this because you don't want to stir up any sediment in the wine. Nor do you want the cork to loosen.

Darkness—Prolonged exposure to sunlight will warm up a bottle of wine. This is why darkness is usually recommended as a condition for storage. However, room lights will not affect a wine.

Humidity—Cool air is moist air, so if the temperature of your storage area is low, the humidity should be just right. Generally, humidity conditions that *you* find comfortable are OK for wine. The humidity should be moderate, neither dry nor damp, and consistent throughout the year.

For everyday drinking, keep red wines in a wine rack in your dining room or kitchen, and white wines in the refrigerator. When storing wines, lay them on their sides so the wine is in contact with the base of the cork. This prevents the cork from drying out and shrinking. A tight-fitting cork does not allow air to enter the wine and age it prematurely.

WINE BINS AND RACKS

Some fine clarets and vintage ports are still shipped in wooden crates. You can use these as wine bins by turning them on their sides so the wine is lying on its side. Cardboard cartons are not suited to cellar storage because they can develop mold that may affect the wine through the cork. Also, they collapse if they become damp.

To avoid such problems, store your wines in a bin made from a wooden box. Lay the bottles sideways, stacked tightly in each box. Label each bin with a number or code and keep a record of the wine in each.

A wine rack can be either wood or metal. Some small, ornate racks are intended for the dining room, while others may be built to hold dozens of bottles. These can be attached to the wall of a cellar or closet. Place bottles in the rack with the label on top. This avoids damaging the labels and allows you to read them without disturbing the wine.

CELLAR BOOK

You can keep a cellar book of your own as a record of what you have and have already consumed. Special books are available at wine stores. Record each wine and your impressions of it.

From left to right: Wicker wine carrier for 8 bottles, Wine rack for 12 bottles, candle for decanting wine, cellar book.

YOUR HOME SUPPLY

It's convenient to divide your purchases into two types—wines for everyday drinking and wines for special occasions. These types of wines are described in more detail in other sections of this book.

EVERYDAY DRINKING

Wines in this category can include ordinary table or *jug* wines—generally sold in half- or full-gallon bottles. These need no cellar aging. Otherwise, choose about two dozen bottles from the following types:

Fruity White Wines—Include Liebfraumilch, Yugoslav Riesling, California Colombard and Chenin Blanc, Alsace Sylvaner, Australian Rhine Riesling.

Dry White Wines—Include French Muscadet and White Bordeaux, Italian Frascati and Verdicchio, California Sauvignon Blanc and Australian Semillon.

Light Red Wines—Include French Beaujolais and inexpensive claret, Gamay from California, and rosé from Portugal, France or California.

Full-Bodied Red Wines—Include California Zinfandel, Australian Shiraz, Mâcon Rouge and Côtes du Rhône from France, Italian Chianti and Spanish Rioja.

SPECIAL OCCASIONS

You can choose fine wines for special occasions with some help from your local wine dealer. Keep them in good condition for the recommended times. If you don't want to store a wine, you may have to pay more for it when it is at its peak.

Fine White Wines—Drink these within about five years of production, the year shown on the bottle's label. Dry white wines include Chablis from France, white Burgundy, German Rhine and Mosel wines, and Alsatian wines.

Sweet White Wines—These will keep for a long time. French Sauternes and German Beerenauslese and Trockenbeerenauslese wines can last for 50 years or longer. Generally, your fine, sweet white wines will be at their best within five to 10 years from the date of the vintage.

Fine Red Wines—Unless your wine is from one of the finest vintages, drink claret, Burgundy and good red wines from California, Australia and South Africa within five to 10 years after the vintage date.

Wines that you should keep longer, up to 20 years, include: Barolo and other Italian wines made with the Nebbiolo grape; full-bodied Rhône wines; and some California wines that are heavy and high in alcoholic content.

Sparkling Wines—When champagne and other sparkling wines are sold, they have completed their aging process and are ready for drinking.

Fortified Wines—This is a strong, sometimes sweet, wine with an alcoholic content of about 20%. Almost all fortified wines, including sherry, port and Marsala, are ready for drinking and do not need to be stored for aging. Vintage port needs at least 10 years in a cellar before it is ready to drink.

Serving Wine

Different types of wine are available to be enjoyed before, during and after a meal. There are many rules and conventions about serving wine with food. The most important consideration when serving any wine is to choose one you will enjoy. See pages 104 to 107 about appetizer and dessert wines.

Luncheon Wines—These should complement the food, not overpower it. As a general rule, serve lighter, drier wines before heavier, sweeter wines. Also, a young wine should normally be served before an older one.

Soups, Salads and Appetizers—Consider a light, dry wine, such as Riesling, Chablis, Muscadet or Semillon. A full-flavored meat or chicken soup may be accompanied by a dry sherry.

Fish—Serve a dry white wine like Chablis, Muscadet, Sauvignon Blanc from California or any similar acidic wine.

Strong fish stews, such as *Cioppino* or *Bouillabaisse* are rich in tomato and garlic. These taste wonderful with a light red wine such as a California Burgundy or a red wine from Southwest France.

Chicken and White Meat—Serve these with either red or white wine. If you are using a cream sauce over the meat, a white Burgundy or Semillon is a good accompaniment. With roasted meat or Italian-style dishes, serve a red wine such as Beaujolais or Chianti.

Red Meat and Game—These taste good with all fine red wines. A steak is traditionally served with good claret. Red Burgundy goes well with roast beef. For venison and other flavorful game, try the full-bodied Rhône red wines, like Hermitage or an Australian Shiraz. Barbecued meats require a full-flavored wine like California Petite Sirah or Zinfandel.

Some Taboos—Although there are no rigid rules about serving wines with food, avoid the following combinations. Otherwise, the result is an unpleasant taste in your mouth.

- Mackerel or any oily fish and red wine.
- Chocolate and any wine.
- Vinaigrette salad dressing with any wine.
- Lemon desserts and any wine.
- Rich egg dishes and white wine.

WINE AT THE TABLE

After deciding on the wines to accompany a meal, the next step is to prepare them for the meal. This puts them in peak condition for drinking.

Temperature—Red wines taste best when served at a temperature between 65F and 70F (18C to 21C), sometimes called *cellar temperature*. What we consider *room temperature* is often too warm, about 72F (22C). This can dull the full flavor of a good red wine. If necessary, chill the wine briefly to lower its temperature near 68F (20C). The exception to this rule is a Beaujolais or Gamay. Both taste better when chilled like a white wine.

White wines require chilling before opening. Generally, a two-hour chill is enough, but some people like their white wine a bit colder or a bit warmer. It is better to serve it colder, because the wine will always warm up after it is poured. If necessary, you can chill a white wine in the freezer for 20 to 30 minutes before serving. Don't forget about the bottle. You can expect it to explode if it freezes. Some people keep a bottle of white wine chilled at the table by putting it in an ice bucket filled with ice and water.

Champagne should be chilled to about 45F (7C) to ensure that the bubbles are released slowly and the flavor retained. Use an ice bucket filled with ice and water to keep the temperature down while the bottle is at the table.

Opening the Bottle—Always use a corkscrew to remove the bottle's cork. Corkscrews come in a multitude of shapes and sizes. Each wine drinker has his favorite. Be sure the screw part is long and curled enough to get a grip on the whole cork. Otherwise, the cork could break and fall into the wine.

To open champagne, hold the cork with your thumb while twisting the bottle firmly in one direction to release the pressure *slowly!* This way you won't lose precious gas and flavor in an explosive, frothy pop.

Breathing—Some experts recommend that you let a wine *breathe* before you pour it. What you do is remove the cork and let the bottle sit undisturbed before pouring it. The reaction of the air with the wine is said to affect the taste of the wine.

Some people let a white wine breathe for about 10 minutes. They claim that it makes a fresh, young wine taste less acidic.

Letting a red wine breathe is more confusing. If the wine is very old, letting it breathe too much can ruin it! Avoid such a problem by tasting the wine after opening it. If it is not harsh, recork it and serve it without benefit of breathing. Otherwise, sample it every

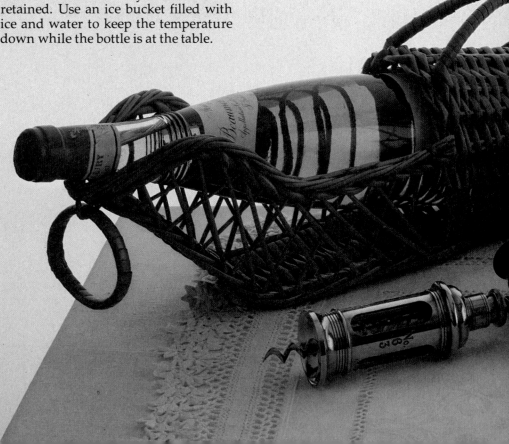

30 minutes. Don't let it breathe for more than two hours. For younger wines, a breathing time from 30 minutes to one hour is usually sufficient.

Decanting—This is pouring the wine into another serving container, such as an attractive crystal decanter. This is useful if you are serving a red wine that has sediment in the bottom of the bottle. Before decanting, let the bottle stand upright for an hour or two. Then pour the wine slowly into the decanter. With a candle or light behind the bottle, watch for the sediment. When it reaches the neck of the bottle, stop pouring.

Pouring—Pour a little wine into the host's glass first. Let him test its quality. Then serve from each person's right. Move clockwise around the table. A standard size bottle of wine—about 25.5 fluid ounces—will serve four to six people.

From left to right:
Wine carrier for a single bottle,
corkscrew,
ship's decanter,
decantavin, a device for
decanting wine,
taster's glass.

2

CHOOSING
WINE

Choosing Bar at the Folies Bergères by
Edouard Manet (1832-1883). Courtauld
Institute, London.

Wines of France

When many people all over the world think of wine, they first think of France. Drinking French wine is like drinking history. Almost 10% of the population of France is connected with the wine business. Much of the annual production consists of ordinary red table wine, *vin ordinaire*, which is most enjoyable when consumed young and fresh.

Some French wines are made at grand *chateâux*, castled estates owned by titled families. Some are made in the *caves* or cellars of the *négociants*, wine merchants who also bottle wines. Small, local growers who don't have wine-making facilities usually send their crops to regional cooperatives to be crushed and fermented, then sold as wine on their behalf.

FRENCH WINE LAWS

At the end of the 19th century, the French wine industry was recovering from a disastrous infestation of a vine louse that destroyed most vineyards. Unscrupulous wine makers were labeling their wines fraudulently. To protect her international reputation, the French government stepped in and created strict laws that controlled various aspects of the industry. Some of the most important ones that help you identify wines are described here.

Appellation Contrôlée (AC)—All fine French wines come from areas controlled by a government body called the *Institut National des Appellations d'Origine (INAO)*. This institute establishes the naming (*appellation*) system for each wine district. Under its guidance, wine makers conform to rules that specify how many vines may be grown per acre, how much wine may

Château Lynch-Bages;
Rosé d'Anjou;
Pouilly-Fuissé 1979;
Veuve Clicquot Ponsardin, Brut;
Bollinger 1975 in champagne bucket.

be made from each acre of vines, and the minimum amount of alcohol in the wine.

About 15% of all French wines are *appellation contrôlee*, coming from areas recognized as producers of top-quality wines. This title is clearly marked on the bottle's label, sometimes with the initials *AC*. Also on the label is the date of the vintage, or year of the grape harvest from which the wine was made.

Vins Délimités de Qualité Supérieur (VDQS)—Wines with the initials *VDQS* on the label are considered good, well-made wines from a particular small region. To win the *VDQS* seal a producer must conform to a set of regulations almost as rigorous as those for the *AC*.

Vin de Pays—Literally, this means *country wine*. They are simple wines that represent the characteristic style of a particular region, which is sometimes named on the bottle.

Vin de Marque—This is wine with a brand name, chosen by the shipper or cooperative that makes the wine. The purpose is to offer the customer a reliable wine that does not vary from year to year. These are usually not vintage-dated because they can be made from blends of wines from different years.

OTHER WORDS YOU'LL SEE ON FRENCH LABELS

Blanc: White.
Cépage: Grape type.
Château: Estate.
Commune: Village or township after which a wine is named.
Demi-sec: Medium-sweet.
Doux: Sweet.
Mise en bouteilles au château: Estate-bottled.
Mousseux: Sparkling. It is used for wines other than champagne.
Propriétaire: Owner of the property and wine-making business.
Récolte, millésime: Vintage.
Rouge: Red.
Sec: Dry.
Supérieur: This usually means the wine is more alcoholic than the ordinary local wine.
Vendange tardive: Late-harvest grapes.

BURGUNDY

The heart of Burgundy is contained in an area called the Côte d'Or, about 270 miles southeast of Paris. Lovers of fine Burgundy will pay any price for a bottle of their favorite Burgundian *cru*. Critics claim that the rarity of some wines has led to merchants charging inflated prices for them.

One straightforward explanation for the high prices is that the vineyards are very small and the region is so far north as to make the climate unpredictable.

Many people own small vineyards in Burgundy. Each vineyard is called a *climat*. It usually forms part of a larger *domaine*, or property. In addition to the *proprietaire récoltant*, the property owner who makes wine himself, there are many *négociants* who blend and sell wines from their cellars. They are usually located in a large town like Beaune.

Because the wine-making activity in Burgundy is much more complex than in Bordeaux, some people choose their wines according to the name of the vineyard. However, there are so many producers that it is best to rely on the name of the shipper when searching for a quality wine. The name of the shipper is usually printed on the label.

Some well-known Burgundy shippers include Louis Latour, Jadot, Joseph Drouhin, Bouchard Père et Fils, Chanson, Patriarche, Charles Vienot, and Jaboulet-Vercherre. Wines exported by these firms represent the particular qualities of the *commune* or *climat* named on the label.

GRAPE VARIETIES

The Côte d'Or is usually divided into two separate districts—Côte de

Nuits, famous for red wines, and Côte de Beaune, famous for white wines. The entire area is in the form of a ridge, consisting mainly of limestone. There is some clay mingling with the limestone soil in the Côte de Nuits.

The Côte de Beaune is purer limestone, with chunks of chalk scattered over the soil. These are ideal conditions for certain grape varieties to flourish. Wine makers all over the world seek out similar soil to cultivate similar vines in the hope that they can make their own "Burgundies."

The Pinot Noir grape is used to make the robust red wines. For white wines the Chardonnay grape is used. Both are delicate varieties that cannot yield heavy crops. The yield is strictly controlled by the *INAO*, so each vineyard earns the right to the *AC* of that area.

Côte de Beaune 1978;
Meursault 1977;
Nuits-St.-Georges 1978;
Pommard Epenots 1971.

CÔTE DE BEAUNE

Pommard is a "velvety" red wine made in a commune on the Côte de Beaune. Despite its well-deserved reputation, it is not the finest red wine of the area. That distinction belongs to Le Corton. Any Burgundy with *Le* plus the *appellation* is the finest of its category. Lesser wines have longer versions of the name, such as Aloxe-Corton.

In addition to the good but often overpriced Pommard, other communes in the Beaune region are Beaune, Pernand-Vergelesses, Aloxe-Corton, and Savigny-les-Beaune. When choosing a wine from this illustrious area, rely on the name and reputation of the shipper to guide you. Some names are mentioned earlier. Most of them are based in the attractive medieval town of Beaune.

Two famous names in white Burgundy are Montrachet and Meursault. Although these communes are very close to each other on the Côte de Beaune, their wines are distinctly different. Montrachet is considered subtle and complex. Meursault tastes heavier and has a buttery flavor.

Fine wines with similar characteristics to Le Montrachet include Chevalier Montrachet, Bâtard Montrachet and Puligny Montrachet. The next level down from these elegant wines are those labeled *premier cru*. They are also slightly lower in price than the *grands crus*. Wines with just a commune name and no vineyard mentioned on the label are the best values.

CÔTE DE NUITS

This area includes many famous communes. To the north are Fixin, Gevrey Chambertin, Chambolle-Musigny and Vougeot. From each comes a memorable red wine, notably Le Musigny and Le Chambertin.

To the south of these is the best known village of all—Vosne-Romanée. A mere four acres of land here produce the legendary *crus* of Romanée Conti. One special feature of the vineyards is that they escaped the ravages of the vine louse *phylloxera*, which destroyed essentially all European vineyards in the 19th century. Romanée-Conti can therefore boast pre-*phylloxera* vines.

The major *crus* here are called Romanée-Conti, La Tâche, Romanée St. Vivant, and Richebourg. Close by is the town of Nuits St. Georges, a commune name you'll find on many pleasant red Burgundies.

Vin ordinaire of Burgundy bears the *appellation Bourgogne*, either *Blanc* or *Rouge*. Although these are variable in quality, sometimes they are good.

CHAMPAGNE

Throughout the world, the name *champagne* is used to mean a particular type of wine—an elegant, sparkling, and expensive liquid used for celebrations. The wine makers of Champagne are dismayed by this. To them, and the laws of France, champagne is a very special sparkling wine made according to age-old traditions in one small part of France, northeast of Paris near Reims.

GRAPE VARIETIES

The northern vineyards of the Champagne region have never made good wine. The Chardonnay, the grape variety for white Burgundies, and its sister grape, the Pinot Noir, do well on the limestone soils of Champagne. However, they rarely ripen fully to develop a rich, balanced flavor. The answer to this problem was to make a special type of wine—one with sparkle.

THE CHAMPAGNE METHOD

The idea of a sparkling wine was familiar to wine makers in Champagne from the earliest days of Roman occupation. . During the warm days of spring, yeast in wine made in the previous autumn would begin fermenting again after the long cold winter. This *secondary fermentation* often left carbon dioxide bubbles in the wine. Many wine makers tried to eliminate this because sometimes the corked bottles exploded.

Some thought the sparkle in the wine improved it. For them, the problems were how to control the secondary fermentation and how to keep the bubbles in the bottle. According to legend, the first man to solve both problems was Dom Pérignon, cellarmaster of the Hautvillers Abbey near Epernay in the Champagne region.

He transferred the newly fermented wine to bottles and added yeast and sugar. He corked each bottle and set it aside in a cool cellar until a secondary fermentation took place. The added yeast and sugar encouraged a vigorous secondary fermentation, creating a lot of carbon dioxide gas. Because the bottle was tightly corked, the gas could not escape. Instead, it dissolved into the wine, waiting to bubble up when the bottle was opened.

To seal the bottles tightly, Dom Pérignon invented the modern style of champagne cork and tied it down into position. He also pioneered the use of strong bottles able to withstand the severe pressure created inside the bottle.

Thus champagne was born. Several years of aging after the secondary fermentation lent additional flavor and character, as the young champagne rested on the *lees*, the sediment of spent yeast cells. One final problem remained, and Dom Pérignon did not have an answer to this—how to remove the sediment without clouding the champagne?

Another process was invented by Veuve Clicquot to solve this problem. Madame Clicquot, who ran champagne behind the British lines during the Napoleonic Wars, was the widow of a champagne maker. Her process, called *rémuage*, involves a gradual turning of each bottle during upside-down storage. The sediment gradually sinks as a plug in the neck of the bottle. The cork is removed and the sediment poured out. The bottle is recorked.

This method is called *méthode champenoise*. Even today each stage is done by hand with painstaking skill and care. Naturally, this involves much time and money, making the price of fine champagne inevitably high.

CHAMPAGNE TYPES

All true champagne is made by the same method. The differences between champagnes occur during bottling. Today, the lees is removed by freezing the neck of the bottle. When the cork is removed, the frozen sediment and a small amount of frozen champagne

Moët & Chandon;
Bollinger 1975;
Veuve Clicquot-Ponsardin, Brut 1973.

goes with it. Then a small amount of old wine mixed with cane sugar, the *dosage*, is added, depending on the sweetness required of the final wine. This is necessary because all of the natural sugars were consumed during fermentations. If no *dosage* were added, a very dry champagne would result.

The types of champagnes most widely available include:

Brut—Very dry, with typical *dosage* of 0.5%.

Extra Dry—Not as dry as Brut, with typical *dosage* between 1 and 2%.

Demi-Sec—Slightly sweet and dry, with typical *dosage* between 4 and 6%.

Doux—Sweet, with typical *dosage* between 8 and 10%.

Pink Champagne—This is made by blending in a bit of local red wine for color. It is made in small quantities in the village of Bouzy.

One interesting aspect of all French champagnes is that most are made from a high proportion of black grapes, pressed so no color is extracted from the skins. The grapes used are the Pinot Noir and Pinot Meunier. Some wine from the white Chardonnay is also blended into a mixture of wines that become champagne. This mixture is called the *cuvée*. Some special champagnes you may see include:

Blanc de Blancs—Only white Pinot Chardonnay grapes are used. It is considered very delicate and fine.

Blanc de Noirs—This is a connoisseur's champagne made from only the black Pinot Noir. It is heavier than a Blanc de Blancs.

Crémant—Due to the use of less yeast and sugar in the secondary fermentation, there is less sparkle in this champagne than the regular type

Vintage-Dated Champagne—Champagne with a date printed on the label usually costs more than non-vintage types. This is because it has been chosen by the champagne maker to be aged for a longer period in his cellars. Vintage champagne is made only in good years, not every harvest.

CHAMPAGNE HOUSES

There are many famous names associated with champagne. Good champagne is also made by small independent growers and cooperatives. However most champagne available for export comes from a few top *maisons*, or houses. These include Bollinger, Krug, Lanson, Veuve Clicquot-Ponsardin, Pol Roger, Taittinger, Moët & Chandon, Heidsieck Monopole, Perrier-Jouët, Laurent Perrier, and Piper-Heidsieck.

MOSEL-SAAR-RUWER

Some people know this area as Mosel, but due to the 1971 wine laws, the official name of the area for wine labels is Mosel-Saar-Ruwer. Wines made here are light, fruity and charming. Because of the region's climate, the grapes can be more acidic than grapes from other regions. This happens when the grapes do not ripen fully.

The principal river in the area is the picturesque Mosel. The other two rivers, the Saar and Ruwer, are much smaller. Wines from these areas are usually called Mosels too. All Mosel wines are distinguished by their green bottles, instead of the traditional German brown bottle.

GRAPE VARIETIES

The Riesling grape is the most popular type here. Although the climate can be cruel and mean the loss of a whole harvest, in good weather the Riesling matures into a wonderfully flavorful fruit.

For the finest wines, wine lovers choose those made from the slate vineyards of the Middle Mosel. The river banks are very steep and difficult to cultivate, but growers in the region have perfected their craft. They are aided by the slate-like soil, which drains well. It dries rapidly and holds together well. The banks, which are as high as 700 feet, face south and southwest and catch the elusive sun.

MOSEL

Many different wines are made in Mosel, but those listed here are among the best available for export.

Trittenheim—This is a southern Mosel town with some fine vineyards making fresh, zesty wines. Vineyard names to look for include Apotheke and Altärchen.

Piesport—Wine lovers from all over the world know this name. Many wines made here are good and inexpensive. But like some fine white Burgundies, their popularity can make

Bereich Beernkastel, 1978 QbA;
Piesporter Goldtröpfchen, Riesling,
   1978 QbA;
Zeller Schwarze Katz 1979;
Trittenheimer Altärchen, Riesling
   Auslese, 1979 QmP.

their authenticity questionable. Avoid this problem by looking for the name of a vineyard on the label.

Piesporter Michelsberg is a pleasant, inexpensive wine. It is named after a *grosslage*, a group of small vineyards. Another famous wine is Piesporter Goldtröpfchen, which means *drops of gold*. In good years, this is an exquisite wine with a special honey-like flavor.

Bernkastel—This is the general name for a large area of the finest Mosel region. Wines may vary in quality from pleasant and drinkable to rare and expensive. Generally, they are drier than other Mosel wines.

Bereich Bernkastel is a wine that comes from the general area. It is a blended wine, usually low-priced. Bernkasteler Badstube and Bernkasteler Kurfurstlay are *grosslage* names for the product of several vineyards. Some are excellent values. Bernkasteler Doktor is an example of a rare, fine Mosel from a single vineyard.

Graach—Some experts considered the village a top-quality producer. Recommended vineyards include Abtsberg,

Heiligenhaus, Monch and Himmelreich.

Wehlen—Top-quality wines also come from this small village. Look for these vineyards—Abtei, Lay, Sonnenuhr, and Rosenberg.

Zeltingen and Zell—These two areas have a variety of wines—some fine, some ordinary. Most wines from this area are slightly sweet. At Zell the best-known wine is called Schwarze Katz. Look for the black cat on the label.

SAAR

When the weather is good for grapes, this region produces some of the region's finest wines. However, in bad years the wine needs extra sugar or blending to become drinkable.

Ockfen and Ayl—The most exciting wines from this area are Ockfener Bockstein and Ayler Kupp.

RUWER

Good wines from this region are less alcoholic than other Mosels. They are described as lighter and softer.

Kasel—The small vineyards around this village are among the best known in the area. One vineyard is Nieschen.

Maximin Grünhaus—This is the name of the vineyard that produces the wine. The vineyard name is so famous that the village name, Mertesdorf, is not used on the label. Wines from this hidden corner of the Ruwer have a fresh taste that is slightly acidic. Wine-label collectors prize its attractive labels.

SPAIN

Not many years ago, Spain was known to many wine drinkers as the source of sherry and inexpensive table wines. Today the picture is different. Top-quality wines from Rioja and Panadés are impressing connoisseurs everywhere. Spain's wine industry is making tremendous efforts to keep up with modern demands.

SPANISH WINE LAWS

Spain has realized the value of control. The Spanish *Denominacion de Origen* is roughly equivalent to the French *appellation contrôlée* and the Italian *DOC*.

Areas selected for this status include the Navarra and Rioja regions of the north, where the finest red wines of Spain are made. Rioja wines are aged in wood for several years before being bottled. Even the youngest must spend at least two years in oak casks to qualify for the *Denominación de Origen*.

GRAPE VARIETIES

Grapes grow almost everywhere in Spain. Most prevalent in the stony, mountainous northern regions of Navarra and Rioja are the red Garnacho grape, related to the Grenache of southern France, and the red Graciano, a native grape. White wines of this area are made from the Malvasia and Viura grapes.

To the east of the Navarra vineyards are those of Panadés in Catalonia. Thanks largely to the efforts of one producer, wines from this region are now widely recognized as equally good to those of the Rioja. The grapes used are much the same. Very good sparkling wines from this area, made with the *méthode champenoise*.

The other principal wine region of Spain is La Mancha. Grapes used are Cencibal, Monastrel and Tintorera for red wines and Lairen for white wines.

RIOJA

One of the reasons this region produces such good wine is that many French wine makers came here when their vines were destroyed by the vine louse in the late 19th century. Many of these wine makers eventually left, but they left behind expertise.

This region has many *bodegas* making good dry red wines. These are aged in wooden casks before being bottled. To determine the age of a Rioja wine, look at the date on the label. If it is a particular year, such as 1976, then the wine is mainly from that year and possibly "topped up" with a little wine from another vintage. If it says 4 *año* or 5 *año*, the wine aged in casks for four or five years and then bottled.

Marqués de Murrieta 1978;
Imperial 1970;
Marqués de Riscal 1978;
Federico Paternina 1976.

The style of good red Rioja is similar to a French claret. It is rich, dry, and full-bodied. White Rioja resembles white French Burgundy in flavor, due to the aging of the wine in wooden casks. This gives them a special butter-like flavor.

Some shippers to look for on labels of good Rioja include Marqués de Riscal, Marqués de Murrietta, Federico Paternina, Bodegas Riojanas, Bodegas Bilbainas and Bodegas Olarra.

CASTILE

The best-known wine of this region is Vega Sicilia. Although it has an Italian-sounding name, it is definitely Spanish. Wines are aged for a minimum of 10 years before being bottled at the bodega near the town of Pena-fiel. The result is a full-bodied dry red wine with a complex flavor.

CATALONIA

This region on the coast of the Mediterranean Sea includes the city of Barcelona.

Perelada—Pleasant red and white wines are made here. In addition, it makes some good sparkling wine with the *bulk* process. This is letting the secondary fermentation occur in a vat instead of the bottle.

Tarragona—A selection of wines is made here, including wine-based liqueurs and vermouths. The local wines are used to make bottled *sangria*, a red wine mixed with citrus juices.

Priorato—This town is mainly known for the dark-red wines that are exceptionally strong and powerful.

Panadés—The Torres family owns this area's best bodega and has an international reputation for quality. Their Vina Sol white wine is excellent, as is their Gran Coronas red wine.

San Sadurni de Noya—The town is the center for quality sparkling wines, including those labelled Codorníu and Freixenet.

LA MANCHA

The vast fertile plain made famous by Cervantes' novel *Don Quixote* is a wine-producing area. Most of the wines produced here go to France and Germany for blending.

Valdepenas—Red and white table wines produced here bear the name of the town. Some are good "jug" wines.

SANTA CLARA & MONTEREY

Paul Masson California Red Wine;
The Firestone Vineyard Chardonnay 1979;
Ridge Zinfandel 1978;
Chalone Vineyard Pinot Blanc 1978.

Almadén Vineyards — This large winery is one of the leading producers of Californian wine, with an annual volume of over 15 million gallons. The Almaden wine list is extensive and includes several highly successful jug wines and more expensive varieties and sparkling wines. Mountain White and Mountain Red jug wines are good value.

Calera — Fine Pinot Noir is made in small quantities.

Chalone — The county's oldest winery, it makes some exceptionally fine wines. Its Chardonnay, Pinot Blac and Pinot Noir fetch high prices but are well worth trying if you want to experience how good a Californian wine can be.

Paul Masson — Even though this winery is owned by the world's largest liquor company its wines are not just large production blends. The selection of dessert, aperitifs, and red and white varieties includes several quality wines from Monterey vines. There are also some house names for varietal wines such as Emerald Day made from Emerald Riesling grapes. Some pleasant jug wines are available in attractive carafes. Its champagne is made by the transfer process.

Ridge Vineyards – A group of Stanford professors owns this winery, which sits spectacularly atop a peak in the Santa Cruz Mountains. It is chiefly known for its full-bodied Zinfandel.

SANTA YNEZ

The region surrounding the towns of Santa Ynez and Solvang, not far from scenic Santa Barbara, is one of California's most recent additions to the wine industry. Production is small but of quality. Wineries include Firestone, Sanford and Benedict, and Zaca Mesa.

CENTRAL CALIFORNIA

Central California has a virtual sea of vines stretching for miles. Most of the production here is in the form of jug wines. Firms like Gallo and Franzia are enormous wine producers with giant wineries resembling oil refineries. These large wineries produce some very pleasant varietals, too. They use the very latest wine making techniques involving careful temperature control to keep the maximum flavour and freshness in the wine.

Delicato Vineyards – The family winery produces table and dessert wines for everyday consumption. The family name is actually Indelicato, but for obvious reasons the name of the winery is slightly different.

Franzia – Like other central California wineries, it offers a selection of generic, appetizer and dessert wines. It recently introduced some varietals.

E & J Gallo — Ernest and Julio Gallo have created the world's largest wine company. The different fruit and grape wines made under Gallo supervision represent one-third of California's wine production. Wine under the Gallo label are good jug and everyday wines. These include Hearty Burgundy and Chablis Blanc. The company offers a selection of varietals such as Sauvignon Blanc, Zinfandel and Ruby Cabernet.

Giumarra — Varietal wines are produced here from grapes grown farther south, near Bakersfield. Red wines include Cabernet Sauvignon and some white varietals such as French Colombard and Chenin Blanc.

Guasti — Wines using this label name are made by the large California Wine Association. Their wines include some well-made varietals and typical white and red jug wines.

CALIFORNIA WHITE GRAPES AND WINE

The white grapes of California that makes the best wine seem to do best in the cool parts of the State. Among the most important are:

Chardonnay: Many connoisseurs claim this grape produces California's most successful white wines. At its finest, varietal Chardonnay is fragrant and memorable. This acclaim has led to high prices and some poor wine selling on the strength of the name alone.

Chenin Blanc: A white jug and varietal wine, it is fruity and medium-sweet. The best come from Napa and Sonoma.

French Colombard: This grape produces fruity wine, often used for blending because they are relatively high in acidity. It is the most commonly planted white variety in the state because it yields a prolific crop.

Fumé Blanc: Sauvignon Blanc grapes yield this crisp, dry white wine. The name was first used in the late 1960's when market research showed that American consumers had difficulty in pronouncing the name of the grape.

Riesling: Any wine containing a variety of Riesling grape can be called Riesling. This makes it less expensive than Johannisberg Riesling. Many Riesling wines contain a high proportion of Grey Riesling and are made medium-sweet.

Sauvignon Blanc: This popular dry white wine has a distinctive flavour of green pepper. In California it can also be known as Fume Blanc. Like Chardonnay, the best Sauvignon Blanc is aged in oak barrels, a rare practice with white wines.

Vermouth—The origins of vermouth are in herbal medicine, when wine was blended with herbs and aromatic extracts. The name Vermouth is derived from *wermut*, a German word for wormwood. Its bitter-tasting flowers are used in vermouth.

Today, vermouth is made by adding brandy to light wine, then flavoring it with a mixture of up to 50 herbs. Each vermouth manufacturer has his own special recipe.

Not long ago, a French vermouth was considered a dry white style. An Italian vermouth was a sweeter red blend. These countries now make both styles, in addition to medium-sweet *bianco* and a rosé vermouth. Other wine-making nations also produce vermouth.

DESSERT WINES

Most dessert wines are sweet. They can be consumed with fruit, cheese, a creamy dessert, or all by themselves. Generally, red dessert wines are best at room temperature. White and brown dessert wines are good when chilled.

Port—The British take credit for inventing this fortified wine. According to one story, Portuguese wine shipped to England spoiled during the voyage. One shipper added brandy to the wine in an attempt to preserve it. The result was a much-improved product.

It is a rich, full-bodied fortified wine made in red, white, and amber colors. True port from Oporto, Portugal is widely imitated but not yet duplicated. To make port, fermentation of the original wine is halted with brandy. Then the young port is aged in wooden casks for two or more years. This mellows the flavor of the wine. These "wood" ports are described on the label as *Ruby* or *Tawny*. Tawny port is older, browner, and less fruity than Ruby port. It is usually more expensive too.

The best port, called *Vintage*, is bottled after aging in a wooden cask for two years. Then it ages in the bottle for at least 10 years. Vintage port is made from the best grapes of good harvests. Famous brands of vintage port include Warre, Dow, Cockburn and Croft.

Some California wineries make excellent ports. The wine makers use the same grape varieties planted in the Douro region of Portugal. Some good brands of California port include Ficklin, Paul Masson, J.W. Morris and Woodbury. Other countries making pleasant port-style wines are Australia and South Africa.

Marsala—Sicily is the home of this sweet fortified wine. It is dark brown and has an alcoholic content between 18 and 20%. One grade of Marsala, *Speciali*, is flavored with egg, almonds, or strawberries.

Muscat Wines—The scented, fragrant muscat grape is made into dessert wines all over the world. Not all are fortified. Some have high alcoholic content because of the high sugar content in the ripe grapes.

In California and Australia, a wide range of Muscat dessert wines are made. These include dark Muscatel made from Black Muscat grapes, and golden Muscatels made with the Muscat of Alexandria grape.

Widmer Port;
Marsala all'uovo;
Muscat de Beaumes de Venise;
Cockburn's Special Reserve Port.

The fortified Muscat de Frontignan and Muscat de Beaumes de Venise made in the South of France are delicious with fruit.

Tokay—The original Tokay is a sweet wine from Hungary, never fortified. However, in California this name is used for a sweet, port-style drink made with a blend of California port, sherry and Angelica, a pale fortified wine made from white grapes.

Index

ACKNOWLEDGMENTS

I would like to thank the following individuals and organizations for their kind assistance in making this book:
Australian Wine Centre, London; Chinacraft Ltd., London; Nicholas Clarke, MW, Henry C. Collison & Sons Ltd, London; Aldwyn Cooper, Covent Garden General Store, London; Richard Dare Kitchen Utensils, London; Del Monico Wines Ltd., London; Julie Fitzherbert-Brockholes; German Food and Wine Centre, London; German Wine Information Service, London; Grierson-Blumenthal Ltd., London; Tony Laithwaite, Sunday Times Wine Club, London; Geoffrey Roberts Ltd., London; The Wine Institute, San Francisco; The Wine Society, London.

Picture Credits:
Anthony Blake, 11; Cooper Bridgeman, 8-9, 22-23; Werner Forman Archive, 10 (bottom left); Fotomas Index, 10 (top left); John Topham, 6; John Yates, 81; California Wine Institute, 13. All other photos by Peter Myers. Illustrations by Elaine Keenan. Maps and diagrams by Chris O'Connor.

PRINTED IN BELGIUM BY
proost
INTERNATIONAL BOOK PRODUCTION